101 American English Idioms

Harry Collis

Illustrated by Mario Risso

Mc Graw Hill

New York   Chicago   San Francisco   Lisbon   London   Madrid   Mexico City
Milan   New Delhi   San Juan   Seoul   Singapore   Sydney   Toronto

23 24 25 26 27 28 29 30 31 32 33   DOC/DOC   0 9 8 7 (0-8442-5446-0)
6 7 8 9 10 11 DOC/DOC 1 5 4 3 2 1   (0-07-148773-5)

ISBN-13: 978-0-8442-5446-3 (book alone)
ISBN-10:   0-8442-5446-0 (book alone)

ISBN-13: 978-0-07-148772-6 (book and CD set)
ISBN-10:   0-07-148772-7 (book and CD set)

ISBN-13: 978-0-07-148773-3 (book for set)
ISBN-10:   0-07-148773-5 (book for set)

Library of Congress Catalog Card Number: 85-62572 (0-8442-5446-0)
Library of Congress Control Number: 2006931803 (0-07-148772-7)

McGraw-Hill books are available at special quantity discounts to use as premiums and sales promotions, or for use in corporate training programs. For more information, please write to the Director of Special Sales, Professional Publishing, McGraw-Hill, Two Penn Plaza, New York, NY 10121-2298. Or contact your local bookstore.

This book is printed on acid-free paper.

Contents

Foreword

Nonnative speakers of English can reach a point in their knowledge of the language where they feel comfortable with standard literary speech; however, they're liable to find themselves in hot water when confronted with idiomatic expressions. When hearing an idiom or colloquialism they may feel frustrated and confused, since the true meaning of the idiom generally cannot be determined by a knowledge of its component parts. In many cases an attempt on the part of the learner to tie down a definition of an idiom that would work in all instances is a futile undertaking.

When used by native speakers, idioms sound natural and fit the occasion, since Americans instinctively feel the imagery and impact of what they are saying. A nonnative speaker of English, on the other hand, may know the basic meaning of such expressions as "I gave it my best shot" or "dressed to kill," but still not be able to use them appropriately. For example, if at a formal gathering an American says to the wife of a foreign diplomat that her gown is elegant, or that she looks lovely, and in appreciation for the compliment her answer is, "Thank you, I gave it my best shot!" or "Thanks, I dressed to kill!", the chances are that the American would be trying his hardest to hold back peals of laughter. Even with a fairly accurate idea of the meaning of an idiomatic expression, the nonnative lacks the intuitive feel for its impact or for the "picture" it creates.

101 American English Idioms is designed to help bridge the gap between "meaning" and "thrust" of American colloquialisms by providing a situation and a graphic illustration of that situation, so that the imagery created by the expression can be felt, rather than simply learned as a stock definition.

The book is divided into nine sections. The title of each section reflects a notion or a manifestation of the physical world, the world of behavior, or the world of the senses with which the reader may easily identify.

It is hoped that the natural tone of the language of the situations in which the idiom is presented will help to convey the *feeling* of the idiom and the circumstances under which it may be used. The illustrations graphically depicting the meaning of the components of the expressions not only add an element of humor, but also serve to highlight the contrast between the literal and actual meaning of the idioms as presented in the text.

An index is included to facilitate recall and location of the expressions.

101 American English Idioms is intended primarily for all students of English. Nevertheless, because of the graphic humor of the idioms in caricature, native speakers of English will also find the book refreshingly entertaining.

Section One

It's a Zoo Out There

Smell a Rat

(feel that something is wrong)

How come the front door is open? Didn't you close it be-
    fore we went shopping?
I'm sure I did. I can't understand it.
Frankly, I **smell a rat**.
Me, too. I'm **convinced that something is definitely
    wrong** here.
We'd better call the police.

Go to the Dogs

(become run-down)

Have you seen their house lately? It's really **gone to the dogs**.

It's true that it has **become run-down and in serious need of repair**, but I'm sure that it can be fixed up to look like new.

I guess with a little carpentry work and some paint it could look pretty decent.

Fishy

(strange and suspicious)

When the security guard saw a light in the store after closing hours, it seemed to him that there was something **fishy** going on. He called the central office and explained to his superior that he thought something **strange and suspicious** was occurring.

Take the Bull by the Horns

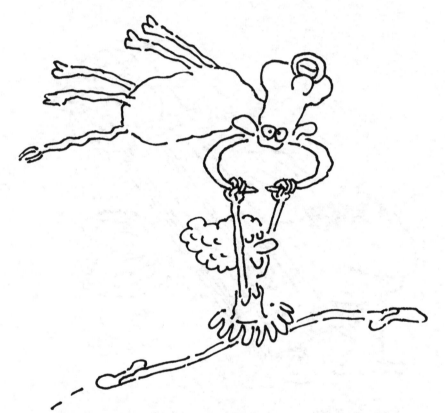

(take decisive action in a difficult situation)

Julie had always felt that she was missing out on a lot of fun because of her clumsiness on the dance floor. She had been putting off taking lessons, but she finally **took the bull by the horns** and went to a professional dance studio for help. She was tired of feeling left out and **acted decisively to correct the situation.**

Horse of a
Different
Color

(quite a different matter)

Eric likes to play jokes on his friends, but he makes sure
that nobody is hurt by any of his pranks. A prank that
hurts someone is a **horse of a different color**! Being
playful is one thing, but hurting someone by one's
prank is **quite a different matter**.

Let the Cat Out of the Bag

(inform beforehand)

Bob was going to retire from teaching in June, and the foreign language department was planning on presenting him with some luggage at his retirement dinner. He wasn't supposed to know about it, but someone **let the cat out of the bag**. At the dinner Bob acted surprised, even though someone **had told him what he was getting before the official presentation**.

For the Birds

(uninteresting and meaningless)

They went to a poetry reading, but they got bored and restless. As far as they were concerned, it was **for the birds**! They left during an intermission because they found the reading **totally uninteresting and meaningless**.

Straight From the Horse's Mouth

(from a reliable source)

How did you find out that Jill was engaged?
I got the information **from a very reliable source**.
You mean Jill told you so herself?
That's right. I got it **straight from the horse's
mouth**!

Horse Around

(play around)

Did you hear about Dave's back injury?
No. How did he get hurt?
Well, after the coach left the gym he decided to stay and
horse around on the parallel bars. He somehow lost
his grip and fell on his back.
That's too bad, but he shouldn't have been **aimlessly
playing around** on the equipment without proper
supervision.

Cat Got Your Tongue?

(can't talk?)

Come on, Connie! Tell us what you think about our little
ride down the rapids yesterday.
Well, uh . . .
Wasn't it exciting?
I, uh . . .
What's the matter? **Cat got your tongue?**
If you must know, I'm **keeping quiet** because I was
scared out of my wits!

Section Two

The Body Has Many Uses

Get in Someone's Hair

(bother someone)

Children! Would you please stop making so much noise!
   And for heaven's sake, pick up your clothes and toys!
   It's hard enough trying to keep this house clean
   without your throwing your things all over the
   place!

Clara, I know that the children **get in your hair**, but
   you should try not to let it upset you so much.

Listen, Jim. I can't help it. The children **bother me and
   make me very angry** when they're so noisy and
   messy.

Shoot Off One's Mouth

(express one's opinions loudly)

Jim doesn't play tennis very much, but he's always **shooting off his mouth** about how good he is. Yet he's fooling nobody. Jim is somewhat of a braggart and everyone knows that he gives opinions without knowing all the facts and **talks as if he knew everything** about the game.

Jump Down Someone's Throat

(become angry with someone)

That's it, Greg! You'd better not come in after midnight again tonight!

I know, dad. You don't have to **jump down my throat**! I told you that I'd make it home around 11:30. I don't intend to be late!

Well, you've said that before and in you come at 2:30 in the morning. You can't blame me for **getting angry and scolding you**. I've got good reason.

Pay Through the Nose

(pay too high a price)

At last Mr. Smith came upon the rare stamp he had been seeking at an auction. Since many other stamp collectors would also be bidding for it, he realized that he would have to **pay through the nose** in order to have it. After considering the increasing value of the stamp, he decided that he would not mind **paying such a high price** for something so rare.

Tongue-In-Cheek

(not serious)

Why were you teasing Sonia about her new hairdo? She
   really took offense at what you said.
I didn't mean to offend her. I was simply making a
   tongue-in-cheek remark when I said that it was
   too elaborate for a girl of her young, tender age.
Well, she thought you were serious. She had no idea that
   you were just saying that **as a joke**.
I'm really sorry. I suppose I owe her an apology.

Pull Someone's Leg

(fool someone)

Hey, Al. I was invited to be a judge for the Miss America
　　Beauty Pageant!
Oh, really? Come on, you're **pulling my leg**!
No, honestly. Do you really think that I'm **trying to
　　fool you with a ridiculous story**?
Well, you've told me foolish stories before.
I can assure you that this one is for real.

Play It by Ear

(improvise as one goes along)

Let's go to the movies, agreed?
Sure. And what'll we do after that?
Oh, I don't know. Let's **play it by ear.**
Well, I would like to have a more definite plan of action.
Don't be like that. It's always more fun **not knowing
    what to expect and deciding what to do as we go
    along**.

Stick Out One's Neck

(take a risk)

How come they're asking me to act as their guide through the jungle?

Evidently they think you're the only one who can lead them to the lost temple.

That jungle has danger lurking around every corner. Why should I **stick my neck out** for them? They didn't pay me for my services.

They know that you would be **taking a great risk and could possibly get hurt**, but you're the only one with enough knowledge to take them to their destination. I'm sure you'll be amply rewarded.

Shake a Leg

(hurry!)

Mary, you always take such a long time to put on your
  makeup. Come on, **shake a leg**!
I'll be finished in a minute. Be patient.
You've got to **hurry** or else we won't arrive on time to
  see the last show.

All Thumbs

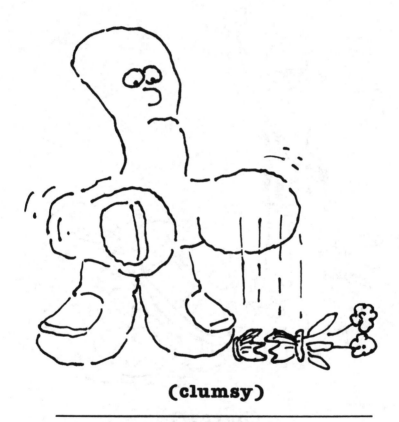

(clumsy)

Hey, Bea. Can you help me out? I don't seem to be able to
button up the back of my dress.

Sure. Let's see if I can do it for you.

I guess I'm **all thumbs** because I'm so nervous. I'm already late for my date.

Well, I suppose that being so nervous would make you
clumsy and awkward. But don't worry. I'm sure
your date will wait.

Not Have a Leg to Stand On

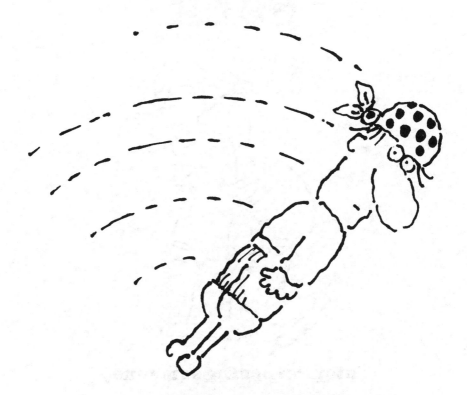

**(to have no good defense
for one's opinions or actions)**

Tom maintains that the firm owes him some back wages
for having worked overtime. However, he **won't have a
leg to stand on** unless he can prove that he put in all
those extra hours. He doesn't stand a chance of getting
his money **without a strong foundation of facts to
support his position**.

Get Off Someone's Back

(stop bothering someone)

Hey, John. I'm bored. Come on, let's go out and do
    something.

Sorry, I'm right in the middle of studying for a physics
    exam. I won't be able to make it tonight.

You've been studying for a long time. Why don't you take
    a break? Come on! Let's go! Forget studying for a
    while!

Look! **Get off my back!** I can't go anywhere!

OK. I'll **stop bothering you** only if you promise to let
    me know the minute you're finished.

Section Three

That's Not Nice

Drive Someone Up a Wall

(annoy someone greatly)

Wow! What a great set of drums!

Yeah, they're great, but I can't play on them when my folks are at home. They say I **drive them up a wall** with all the loud banging.

I get the same thing at home. My folks tell me that I **annoy them and get them really angry** whenever I turn up the volume on my stereo.

String Someone Along

(lead someone on dishonestly)

Liz had high hopes of marrying Dean. When he ran off
with another woman, she realized that he was just
stringing her along. She had felt very strongly about
him and was really hurt to see that he was **deceiving
her** and had no intentions of ever marrying her.

Sell Someone Down the River

(betray someone)

I heard that poor Jud landed up in jail.

Yeah. His so-called girlfriend **sold him down the river** and claimed the reward on him.

I can't understand that. I thought she was devoted to him.

She couldn't have been very devoted to him if she **betrayed him and informed the police** about his hiding place.

That just goes to show you what people will do for money.

Leave Someone High and Dry

(abandon someone)

Say, Jill. I thought that John was going to help you do
the dishes tonight.

So did I. But he **left me high and dry**.

Where did he go?

Well, he got a call from some of his pals at work to go
bowling, and he **left me alone to do all this work
without any help at all**!

Sell Someone Short

(underestimate someone)

Just because he does not say very much is no reason to **sell him short**. Actually, he's a profound thinker and a most talented writer. People tend to **underestimate him and not give him the credit he deserves** because they think he's shy.

Snow Job

(insincere talk)

The salesman tried to convince a group of investors that the properties he was selling would soon be worth much more money than he was asking. However, no one bought anything from him because they felt he was giving them a **snow job**. No one was deceived by his **insincerity and exaggerated claims** about the worth of the properties.

Spill the Beans

(reveal a secret)

Did you know that Harry was going to take Kathy on a Caribbean cruise?

Yes, I did. He was planning on surprising her with the tickets for their anniversary, but someone **spilled the beans**.

What a shame! That was supposed to have been a surprise.

Yes, it's too bad that someone **told her about the trip beforehand** and ruined Harry's surprise.

That's OK. Her enthusiasm was not dampened in the least!

Feed Someone a Line

(deceive someone)

Mr. Jones had been telling Louise how efficient she was and how much he admired her work at the office. He had promised her a promotion in the near future, but she soon discovered that he was **feeding her a line** when he passed her by and gave the promotion to someone less capable. Louise was acutely disappointed to find out that Mr. Jones was **not telling her the truth, and that he was deceiving her**.

Section Four

People Do the Strangest Things

On Ice

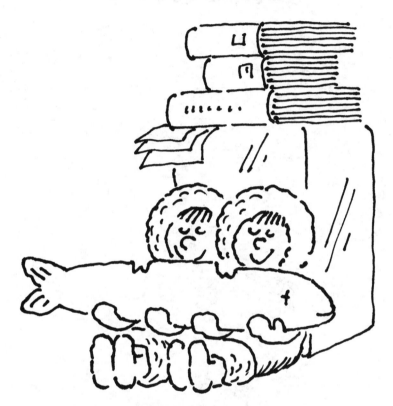

(set aside for future use)

We've been working on this sales report for some time
now. Don't you think we should take a break for some
dinner?

Now that you mention it, I am kind of hungry. Let's put
the report **on ice** awhile and grab a bite to eat.

That's fine. I'd be happy to **stop working on it and set
it aside** until we get some food.

Great! Let's lock up and go.

Shoot the Breeze

(chat informally)

What are you going to be doing this afternoon?
Oh, I don't have anything in particular in mind.
Why don't you come over to my place? We can listen to
some records and **shoot the breeze**.
That sounds OK to me. I'd like to relax listening to music and **visit and chat informally** until my folks
get back from shopping.

Bite the Dust

(go down in defeat)

Andy did exceptionally well in all of the track events, but he **bit the dust** in the high jump competition. Much to the disappointment of his fans, he **went down in defeat**, **losing to a competitor** from the visiting team.

Bend Over Backwards

(try very hard)

When Joan first started teaching she was afraid that
she would have a lot of trouble getting used to the kids
and to the faculty. Her fears turned out to be unfounded,
since everybody **bent over backwards** to help her.
Everyone **tried very hard** to help her feel comfortable
and adjust to the school.

Hit the Hay

(go to bed)

Listen, Kim. We're going to be really busy with moving
    tomorrow, and we've got to get an early start.

I guess you're right. We'll need all the rest we can get.

What do you say we **hit the hay** now?

Agreed. Let's **go to bed** and get a good night's sleep. It's
    going to be a long day.

Cough Up

(give unwillingly)

Say, Greg. Did you finally get that computer that you
   wanted so much?

Not yet. I needed to raise a couple of hundred dollars
   more.

Is it going to take you a while to raise the money?

It would have taken me forever, but dad said he'd **cough
   up** the money I need since I'm going to be using the
   computer for my school work.

Maybe it was **difficult for your dad to give** you the
   money—but then, he knows that it's for a good
   cause.

Jump the Gun

(to be hasty)

Denise was planning on telling her grandparents that the doctor said she was going to have twins, but when her dad found out he **jumped the gun** and told them before Denise could say a word. He was so excited that he **became hasty** and revealed the news before Denise had a chance to tell them.

Scratch Someone's Back

(return a favor)

Hey, Bea. I need some help stacking these boxes. Would
　　you please give me a hand?

OK. And I need some help tidying up the house. How
　　about your helping me out after that?

OK. If you **scratch my back, I'll scratch yours**.

I know you don't like doing housework, but I'll **help you
　　with the boxes if you promise to return the
　　favor**.

No problem. I'll even do the windows.

Hit the Ceiling

(become very angry)

Don's father **hit the ceiling** when he was informed that his son had been detained by the police for disorderly conduct. He **became violently angry**, since he had often warned his son not to keep company with that group of boys.

Fork Over

(hand over, give)

Hey, Dan. How come you're looking so sad?

It's nothing, really. I unexpectedly bumped into Ralph
and he asked me to **fork over** the ten bucks I owed
him.

Did he expect you to pay him back right then and there?

Yes, he did. It was all the money I had, and I had to **hand
it over** to him.

Don't complain. After all, he did you a favor by lending it
to you in the first place.

Turn
Someone Off

(disgust someone)

How was your date with Marty last night?

Well, it started off OK, but he really **turned me off** when
we went for a snack after the movies.

Did he say or do something to annoy you?

Frankly, he **disgusted me** when he tried to talk with
his mouth full.

I don't blame you. That would have really bothered me
too.

Go Fly a Kite

(go away!)

For the past three hours Jerry had been trying to convince Linda to go to the art exhibition with him. She had been refusing all along and finally in desperation she told him, "**Go fly a kite**!" Jerry didn't like to be told to **go away in such a forceful manner**. Nevertheless, he finally stopped trying to get Linda to attend the exhibition.

Kick the Bucket

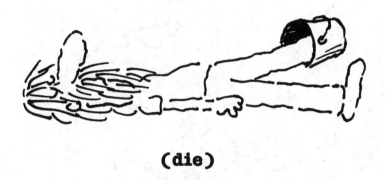

(die)

It's been said that the old man knew of a buried treasure, but he **kicked the bucket** before telling anyone where it was. If the treasure exists, the old man unfortunately took the secret of its location with him when he **died**.

Raise a Stink

(protest strongly)

Listen! Don't try to use any of your sister's clothes
without asking her first. She's liable to **raise a
stink** if she finds something missing.

I'm sure that there will be no problem. She's borrowed
some of my things before, and I've never said anything. I really doubt that she will **protest very
strongly**.

Section Five

Clothes Make the Man (and Woman)

Wet Blanket

(dull or boring person who spoils the happiness of others)

James was not invited to go on the outing with the rest of the group because he's such a **wet blanket**. On many previous occasions he has **kept others from enjoying themselves by his pessimism and lack of enthusiasm**. It's understandable that no one wants him around.

Keep Under One's Hat

(keep something a secret)

Although the contestants were most anxious to know who won the prizes in the piano competition, the judges **kept the results under their hats**. They **kept the results a secret** so that the formal announcements could be made in public at the awards ceremony.

Up One's Sleeve

(concealed)

All right, Sara. We know that you're planning something big for Jean-Paul's birthday. Mind telling us
just what you have **up your sleeve**?

I wanted to make his birthday a very special event.
Jean-Paul has a sister living in France, and I sent
her an airplane ticket so that she could be here for
his birthday.

Boy! That is something special! We kind of guessed that
you had some **concealed plan** and were waiting for
the right time to reveal it.

Well, I didn't want to say anything until I was sure she
could come.

Dressed to Kill

(wear one's finest clothing)

The reception for the new Swedish ambassador at the Jennison's was quite lavish. Naturally, everybody was **dressed to kill**. Since it was a formal occasion, everyone was **dressed in their finest, most elegant clothes**.

Give Someone the Slip

(make a getaway)

The police were chasing the thief through the streets of
the city, but he managed to **give them the slip**. No wonder. There were so many people around that the thief
managed to **escape** by getting lost in the crowds.

Knock Someone's Socks Off

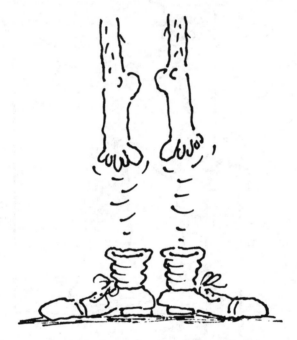

(enthuse and excite)

Hi, John. What's new?

Oh, nothing too much with me, but you ought to see Alfredo's new car. It'll **knock your socks off**!

So, he finally got that Italian sports car he's been dreaming about.

He sure did! When you see all the custom features that it has, you'll **get so enthused and excited** you won't know what to do!

Boy, I can hardly wait to go for a ride in it!

Talk Through One's Hat

(make foolish statements)

We were discussing ethnic traditions and customs with
Fred the other day, and he showed just how little he
knew about other cultures.

What do you mean?

Well, he said that as far as he could tell, there wasn't
much difference in behavior and temperament between the English and the Hispanics.

It's plain to see that he was **talking through his hat**!

True, but Fred thinks he's an authority on everything.
It was difficult to convince him that he was talking
ignorantly. He's got a reputation for **making foolish, inaccurate statements**.

Lose One's Shirt

(lose a great deal of money)

I happened to bump into Doug at lunch yesterday
afternoon.

What's new with Doug these days?

He wasn't doing so well. For one thing, he told me he
lost his shirt at the races.

Doug has always liked to bet on the horses. I'm not surprised that he **lost a great deal of money**.

Yeah. At this rate he'll never have a penny to his name!

In Stitches

(laughing very hard)

Danny was hilarious at the party the other night. He
   had us all **in stitches**! I didn't realize that he was
   such a comedian.
He's always been funny, but last night he outdid himself. He had us **laughing so hard that it hurt our
   sides**.

Dressed to the Teeth

(dressed elegantly)

Did you see Hilda at the party last night?
Yes, I did. She was really **dressed to the teeth**!
Well, she **had on her finest, most elegant clothing**
    because she was out to make a good impression
    on Bill.

Section Six

When Things Go Wrong

Lemon

(something defective)

Have you seen Joanne's new car yet?

Yeah. It looks good, but she's had nothing but problems with it.

That's too bad. It sounds like she got a real **lemon**.

She sure did! No sooner did she drive it home from the dealer's than it **proved defective and started breaking down**.

Out of the Woods

(out of danger)

Although Eric was well on his way to recovering from his bout with pneumonia, he was still not **out of the woods**. The doctors told him that he would have to take it easy and avoid exposure to cold, since he was not **out of danger and difficulty** yet.

Get Up on the Wrong Side of the Bed

(wake up in a bad mood)

What's the matter with Bernard today? He started
  shouting from the moment he stepped into the
  office.
I don't know. He usually doesn't act that way at all. I
  guess he **got up on the wrong side of the bed**.
Just because he **woke up in a bad mood** is no reason
  for him to be so cross and to go around shouting at
  everybody.
Hopefully he'll relax as the day goes on.
Amen!

Out on a Limb

(in a risky position)

The members of the committee realized that their position against expanding the student aid program was an unpopular one, and that they were going **out on a limb** by voting against the program. Nevertheless, their position was justified to a certain extent. Although they knew that they were placing themselves **in a risky position**, they felt that other budgetary considerations were of greater urgency.

Eating
Someone

(bothering or worrying someone)

Hey, Alice. What's been **eating you** lately? Don't you realize how rude and irritable you've become?
I know. I'm really sorry for the way I've been acting.
Well, why don't you tell me what has been **bothering
   and upsetting you** and maybe we can work your
   problem out together.
I'll admit that it would help to talk to someone about it.

Get the Ax

(be dismissed, fired)

I feel sorry for Richard. He was feeling quite depressed
    when I ran into him.

Did he tell you what was bothering him?

Among other things, he informed me that he **got the ax**
    at work.

That's strange. He's always been a conscientious
    worker. I wonder why they **dismissed him from
    his job**?

Evidently he had a disagreement on company policies
    with one of the top executives.

In the Hole

(in debt)

Unfortunately, Peter had to sell his neighborhood hardware store. Because of competition from the bigger stores in the shopping center, he was going **in the hole** every month. His store was small and did not generate enough income to meet expenses. As a consequence, he was rapidly **losing money and going into debt**.

Bite the Bullet

(endure in a difficult situation)

We really had a frightening experience when we went
hunting last month.

What happened?

We got lost in the wilderness and had to **bite the bullet**
until help arrived.

Did you manage OK?

Barely. We weren't prepared for the cold weather and we
couldn't find any shelter. We had to **endure in a
very trying situation**. We almost froze by the time
they found us.

Face the Music

(accept the consequences)

It's no wonder you have a stomachache. I told you not to
eat so many green apples. You don't listen, and now
you're going to have to **face the music**.

The trouble with me is that I can't stop with just one or
two, especially when they're so tart. I'll admit that I
tend to forget that eventually I'm going to have to
accept the consequences for what I've done.

I sure hope it was worth it!

Blow It

(fail at something)

How did you do on the history exam?

I think I **blew it**! There was a section on the Civil War, and that's the chapter in the book that I studied the least.

Well, at this point you can't really be sure that you **completely failed** the examination. You must have done okay on the rest of the test.

Perhaps I didn't fail the entire exam, but I'm sure that I didn't do well.

At the End of One's Rope

(at the limit of one's ability to cope)

The Jones's housekeeper was completely useless! Poor Mrs. Jones felt that she was **at the end of her rope** when she walked into the house and saw the children crying and unfed, dirty dishes in the sink, and clothes strewn all over the place. She had had to leave the house and children in someone else's care while she was off on business. Now that she came back to all of this disorder and disarray, she felt that she had reached **the limit of her ability to cope with the situation**.

On One's Last Legs

(sick and failing)

Poor Mike. He was one of the greatest musicians I've ever known, but when I saw him the other day he looked like he was **on his last legs**.

Yeah. He hardly plays any more.

What made him give up his music?

Apparently he lost confidence in himself at some point in his career, and he's been **sick and failing** ever since.

Hot Under the Collar

(extremely angry)

Did you see how Bill came in to work this morning?
Did I ever! Boy, was he **hot under the collar**!
What brought that on?
He said that he was **extremely angry** because he got
    stuck in slow-moving traffic and arrived late for an
    important business meeting.

On the Line

(in danger of being lost)

Lately Tom's been more conscientious about the accuracy and quality of his work with the company. He was warned that his job was **on the line** because of his lack of concern for his duties. When Tom was alerted that he was **in danger of losing his job**, he began to take his obligations with the company more seriously.

Section Seven

When Things Go Well

For a Song

(for very little money)

Sara, I picked up the perfect chair for the living room the other day.

That's wonderful. I know you've been looking for some time. Where did you finally come across what you wanted?

I was really quite lucky. I got it **for a song** at a little furniture store. I was able to buy it **for very little money** because the owners of the store were right in the middle of their spring liquidation sale.

Make a Splash

(be successful and attract attention)

Do you remember Andre and Jack?

Yes, I do. Weren't they working together on some kind of a novel?

That's right. It was finally published and I understand that it **made quite a splash** both domestically and abroad.

That's great news! They're both talented and hard-working. It's good to hear that the book was so **successful and attracted such a great deal of attention**.

Have the World by the Tail

(be successful and happy)

Marc finished school at the top of his class and he was offered an excellent position with an accounting firm. Now he feels that he **has the world by the tail**. Everything has been working out for him lately, and it's no wonder that he's **feeling so successful and happy**.

Sitting Pretty

(in a fortunate position)

I heard that Michael and Jennifer got a good price when
they sold their house.

Yes, they did. Now they're really **sitting pretty**. As a
matter of fact, they're thinking of going on a long
vacation.

I wish I were **in such a fortunate position**. I haven't
had a vacation in years.

Feel Like a Million Dollars

(feel wonderful)

I bumped into Nick at the barbershop yesterday. He looked great, but I noticed that he had a slight limp when he walked.

I guess you didn't know that he had an operation on his knee.

No, I didn't. How's he feeling?

He says he's **feeling like a million dollars** now. Apparently the pain in his knee is all gone.

It's good that he's **feeling so wonderful**. It must be a refreshing change not having to put up with all that discomfort.

Kick Up One's Heels

(celebrate)

The prerequisites for admission to the Theater Arts School are quite demanding, and those students who were finally accepted had reason to **kick up their heels**. It was only natural that those who made it through the exams and interviews would want to **celebrate the occasion by going out and having a good time**.

Bury the Hatchet

(make peace)

Somebody told me that you and Doug had been quarreling over the construction site of the new building.

That's true, but we worked out the problem and decided to **bury the hatchet**.

Glad to hear that. You guys have always worked well together.

Well, once we came to the conclusion that we both had the same goal in mind, we **put an end to our bitter feelings and made peace with each other**.

Paint the Town Red

(carouse and have a good time)

How did you enjoy your vacation to Europe last
   summer?

It was marvelous. I'll never forget the time we had when
   we were in Rome. There was no end to things to see
   and do.

And how was the night life?

Great! We **painted the town red** the first three nights
   we were there.

Didn't that get to be pretty expensive?

I guess so, but we were so excited by all that the city had
   to offer that we **went out carousing** without thinking about the cost.

Get Away Clean

(escape punishment)

After robbing a neighborhood bank, the robbers sped off in a waiting car and **got away clean**. In spite of all police efforts to apprehend them, the criminals **were never caught and punished** for their crime.

Come Alive

(brighten up and become active)

Up to now the guests at the party had been eating and
making small talk, but when the rock band arrived,
everyone **came alive**. When the band started playing all
the latest rock hits, everybody **brightened up and became very active**.

Section Eight
Do Your Best

Toot One's Own Horn

(boast)

Michael's last novel was a best seller. He has no need to **toot his own horn** about his literary accomplishments. His readers and critics alike will now become aware of his talent. He won't have to **boast about his skill and success** as a writer.

Stick to One's Guns

(maintain one's position)

In spite of the fact that it was inadvisable to have a controversial figure address the club, the chairman **stuck to his guns** and insisted that it would make good sense to hear the other side of the question before taking a vote on the issue. He **maintained his opinion and position on the matter**, even though a number of members tried to make him change his mind.

Get the Ball Rolling

(initiate action)

Look! You've been talking about repairing the roof for
weeks now. Don't you think it's about time to **get the
ball rolling**?

I know, but I've been busy with other things. I promise
I'll get to it this weekend.

The time to **start doing it** is right now! According to
the weather report it's supposed to rain tomorrow.

Mind One's P's and Q's

(take care in speech and action)

Listen, Larry. If you want an invitation to Clarissa's
    party you'd better **mind your P's and Q's**.
But I haven't been doing anything to offend her.
I'll tell you one thing. You're going to have to **be careful
    of what you say and how you act** around Susan.
Come on! Susan and I are just friends.
I know that, but Clarissa is the jealous type. She's liable
    to think that something is going on between the two
    of you.

Hang On

(persevere)

During the depression years the Smiths had a great deal of trouble with their business, but somehow or other they were able to **hang on**. Although they almost lost their store, they managed to **persevere** until things got better.

Give It One's Best Shot

(try hard)

Can you do anything about repairing this TV set?

I'm not much of an electrician, but I'll **give it my best shot**.

Many thanks. I'd be most appreciative.

OK. I'll **try my hardest** to fix it, but I'm not promising that I'll succeed.

At this point, I'll take all the help I can get.

Make Ends Meet

(pay one's bills)

It's almost impossible trying to keep up with the high
cost of living.

It's true. Things are so expensive nowadays that it's
very difficult to **make ends meet**.

You know, even with Lucie's salary, our combined income is **hardly enough to pay all the bills**.

Get the Jump on Someone

(get the advantage over someone)

Did you have a nice time at the school dance last night?

To tell you the truth, I would have enjoyed myself more
   if I had been able to go with Teresa instead of Elena.

Why didn't you ask Teresa in the first place?

I was about to, but Benito **got the jump on me**.

How did he manage to do that?

He **got the advantage over me** by telling Teresa that if
   she went with him, he'd take her out to dinner and
   then to the dance in his brand new convertible.

Well, now, she can hardly be blamed for accepting an offer like that!

Pull Strings

(exert influence)

Steven had been unsuccessful in getting tickets for the opening game of the season. However, he **pulled some strings** with the manager of the team and got excellent seats. There's no doubt that he got the tickets only by **exerting his influence with a person important enough to help him get what he wanted**.

Spread Oneself Too Thin

(become involved in
too many activities)

Although Teresa has always been an excellent student, her marks have been going down lately because she is **spreading herself too thin**. Besides spending a great deal of time in after-school sports, she got a part-time job as a clerk in a department store. It's only natural that her grades would suffer. She is **becoming involved in so many activities that she cannot devote the time that it takes to excel in any one of them**.

Go to Bat for Someone

(help out and support someone)

Is it true that Don got into some trouble at work last week?

Yes, he did. He was reproached for not turning in his sales reports, but his secretary **went to bat for him**.

What was she able to do?

She **helped him out a great deal** by admitting that she had misplaced the reports that he gave her to be typed.

So, it was her fault, not his.

Right.

Duck Soup

(easy, effortless)

Can you help me hook up my new stereo equipment? I'm
   having quite a bit of trouble with all these con-
   nections.

Sure. That's **duck soup** for me.

Well, with all your experience in electronics, I have no
   doubt that it will be **very easy** for you to do.

No problem. Glad to help out.

Section Nine

You Don't Say

Money Talks

(money can influence people)

We've been waiting for three months to get delivery on
our car, and people who put in their order after us
have already gotten theirs.

Well, **money talks**. Why don't you try giving the dealer a
little something extra to move things along?

I know full well that **money has the power to influence people**, but I refuse to pay extra for a service
that is owed to me as a client.

If you want to have your car maybe you'd better
reconsider.

Let Sleeping Dogs Lie

(do not agitate a potential source of trouble)

You'd better not say anything to the owner of the building about painting your apartment. If I were you I'd **let sleeping dogs lie**. The last time you asked him to do some repairs, he raised your rent.

You're telling me **not to make trouble if I don't have to**, but I'm going to risk making him angry, since I can no longer stand to look at the paint peeling off the walls.

Shape Up or Ship Out

(behave properly or leave!)

Al had been constantly reprimanded for being negligent on the job. Finally, in desperation his supervisor exclaimed, "**Shape up or ship out**!" Al admitted that he had not been taking his work seriously and realized that he should **be more conscientious about his job or he would be discharged**.

If the Shoe Fits, Wear It

(admit the truth)

Joe feels rather badly because he's always being criticized for his sloppy personal appearance.
With reason. "**If the shoe fits, wear it**," I always say.
Still, I can't help feeling sorry for the guy. I know that
**what people say about him is true, and that he
should admit it**. He doesn't seem to want to im-
prove his appearance. Evidently, he himself can't
see anything wrong with the way he looks.

Different Strokes For Different Folks

(everyone has different interests and tastes)

It's hard to understand how Millie and Ron ever got together. She has always gone in for sailing and he can't stand to be on water. He enjoys the opera and she likes jazz.

You know what they say: "**Different strokes for different folks!**"

You don't have to tell me that **everyone has different interests and tastes**. I still can't figure out what attracted them to each other in the first place.

Haven't you heard that opposites attract?

Bark Worse Than One's Bite

(not as bad-tempered as one appears)

On occasion Mr. Hopkins speaks harshly to his students, especially when they fail to complete their homework assignment. Nevertheless, they all know that his **bark is worse than his bite**. He threatens to keep them after school and to inform their parents, but he's **not really as bad-tempered as he appears**.

Eyes Are Bigger Than One's Stomach

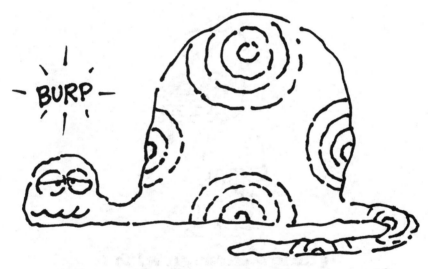

(take more food than one can eat)

Chris, why don't you finish eating that third helping of
   dessert?
I guess my **eyes were bigger than my stomach** when
   I said I wanted more.
I'm not surprised. The same thing happens to me. Some-
   times, when I'm really hungry, I'll **take more food
   than I can possibly eat**.

Put One's Money Where One's Mouth Is

(follow through with a stated intention)

You've been promising to take us to Disneyland for the
past two years. Since the kids are free, how about
putting your money where your mouth is?
You don't have to remind me. I have every intention of
doing exactly what I said I'd do. But you yourself
know that in the past we have been unable to go because of other financial obligations. Things have
eased up and it looks like we'll be able to go this year.

The Early Bird Catches the Worm

(arriving early gives one an advantage)

Marc, the lines for the rock festival are going to be miles long! If you expect to get tickets for you and Marika, remember that old saying, "**The early bird catches the worm.**"

I guess you're right. Marika is looking forward to the concert, and I'd hate to disappoint her. I'll **get up real early to get a place at the head of the line**. That way I'll get the tickets I want, for sure!

People Who Live in Glass Houses Shouldn't Throw Stones

(one should not criticize when one is equally at fault)

Janet has often criticized her friend Lois for driving too fast, yet she herself has had her license suspended for exceeding the speed limit. Lois once tried to tell her that **people who live in glass houses shouldn't throw stones**, but it didn't do much good. Janet simply didn't accept the fact that she **should not pass judgment on other people when she is just as bad as they are**.

All's Well That Ends Well

(a successful outcome is worth the effort)

Hi, Benito. How are things going?

Well, everything's OK now. Remember that teaching job for which I applied?

Yes, I sure do.

Well, I was finally hired, but I had a bit of a rough time before I got it. Between all that paperwork and all those interviews, I'm all worn out. Thank goodness it's all over.

Great! **All's well that ends well.** After all that you went through, I'm happy to hear that **things finally turned out satisfactorily for you.**

Yes. I'm happy, too. It was really worth the effort.

Index to Idioms

H

hang on (persevere) 83
have the world by the tail (be successful and happy) 71
hit the ceiling (become very angry) 39
hit the hay (go to bed) 35
horse around (play around) 9
horse of a different color (quite a different matter) 5
hot under the collar (extremely angry) 67

I

if the shoe fits, wear it (admit the truth) 94
in stitches (laughing very hard) 53
in the hole (in debt) 61

J

jump down someone's throat (become angry with someone) 13
jump the gun (to be hasty) 37

K

keep under one's hat (keep something a secret) 46
kick the bucket (die) 43
kick up one's heels (celebrate) 74
knock someone's socks off (enthuse and excite) 50

L

leave someone high and dry (abandon someone) 26
lemon (something defective) 55
let sleeping dogs lie (do not agitate a potential source of trouble) 92
let the cat out of the bag (inform beforehand) 6
lose one's shirt (lose a great deal of money) 52

M

make a splash (be successful and attract attention) 70
make ends meet (pay one's bills) 85
mind one's P's and Q's (take care in speech and action) 82
money talks (money can influence people) 91

N

not have a leg to stand on (to have no good defense for one's opinion or actions) 21

O

on ice (set aside for future use) 31
on one's last legs (sick and failing) 66
on the line (in danger of being lost) 68
out of the woods (out of danger) 56
out on a limb (in a risky position) 58

P

paint the town red (carouse and have a good time) 76
pay through the nose (pay too high a price) 14
people who live in glass houses shouldn't throw stones (one should not criticize when one is equally at fault) 100
play it by ear (improvise as one goes along) 17
pull someone's leg (fool someone) 16
pull strings (exert influence) 107
put one's money where one's mouth is (follow through with a stated intention) 98

R

raise a stink (protest strongly) 44

S

scratch someone's back (return a favor) 38

sell someone down the river (betray someone) 25

sell someone short (underestimate someone) 27

shake a leg (hurry) 19

shape up or ship out (behave properly or leave!) 93

shoot off one's mouth (express one's opinions loudly) 12

shoot the breeze (chat informally) 32

sitting pretty (in a fortunate position) 72

smell a rat (feel that something is wrong) 1

snow job (insincere talk) 28

spill the beans (reveal a secret) 29

spread oneself too thin (become involved in too many activities) 88

stick out one's neck (take a risk) 18

stick to one's guns (maintain one's position) 80

straight from the horse's mouth (from a reliable source) 8

string someone along (lead someone on dishonestly) 24

T

take the bull by the horns (take decisive action in a difficult situation) 4

talk through one's hat (make foolish statements) 51

tongue-in-cheek (not serious) 15

toot one's own horn (boast) 79

turn someone off (disgust someone) 41

U

up one's sleeve (concealed) 47

W

wet blanket (dull or boring person who spoils the happiness of others) 45